Pure Morning

by

Aaron Powell

This is **not** a work of fiction. Names,
characters, and places, have been
changed to protect the identity of those
of us who were involved.

Also by Aaron Powell:

Doomsday Diaries series

Benjamin

Scream, "Aye, Sir!"

Sugar Baby

Hurry Up and Wait

Gun Control

Priority

C-Town

Voluntary

The Girl from Reading Center

For those of us who survived

"The tragedies of maturer life cannot surpass the first tragedies of youth."

—*Mark Twain*

I wake to the sound of the phone ringing, and I'm instantly aware of the foul taste of vomit and stale cigarettes in my mouth. My tongue is putrid and feels like dry sandpaper as I attempt to wiggle it back to life.

Who is this pretty, young, dark-haired girl lying next to me? Wait, It's Corrine. I'm still dressed, and so is she. We must have passed out like this together.

The phone is still ringing and the answering machine picks up. It's RJ's friend from work. The muffled sound of his voice comes from the other side of my bedroom door. I struggle to get out of bed, and when I stand, I'm lightheaded and topple to the floor.

God, I'm still wasted. What the hell did we get into last night, anyway?

I use the bed to pull myself to my

feet. My vision is blurred.

Come on, Patrick. Gotta wake RJ up for work.

"RJ," I mumble. "Wake up, buddy. Workie-workie."

The answering machine clicks off. Silence.

I press my bedroom door open, stopping in the doorway to get my bearings.

"RJ?"

More silence. An eerie feeling overcomes me as I scan the living room and bring my gaze to rest on the back of our baby-blue couch. Something's...*off*.

Careful to keep my balance, I inch across the living room toward the couch. I start to falter and catch myself, gripping the back of the couch. Then I see him.

"RJ! Hey, buddy, wake up. You're

gonna be late for work."

He's lying on his back, and I reach down with one hand to shake him awake.

"I guess we had a rough night—"

His flesh is cold, and I'm suddenly aware of how blue his lips are.

Something takes over. Instinct? In a flash I'm around the couch. I've pushed the coffee table away, and I'm kneeling before him. I try to shake him awake. His tongue is visible through his lips, and I don't think he's breathing. I use my thumb to depress his tongue so I can give him mouth-to-mouth, but a bloody discharge seeps out, coating my thumb. I'm really starting to panic. I try to turn him on his side, but he's so fucking heavy. I finally manage, and as I turn his body toward me, more of the fluid pours out of his mouth and dribbles onto the couch and carpet.

"No, no, no, no, no, buddy! Please wake up!"

I'm losing touch with reality, if I ever *was* in touch. Is this real? Is this a fucking nightmare?

Please, God, let this be a nightmare.

RJ's shirt collar looks too tight. I try to tear it away from his body, but my arms are weak and feel foreign to me. I scramble to my feet and move to the kitchen counter. I find a knife resting beside a pile of crushed pink pills. The kitchen is littered with beer cans and a couple of half-empty liquor bottles. A gravity bong floats in the sink. I grab the knife and rush back to RJ's body, and I realize that there are little blue pills scattered on the living room floor. My head is drifting in a fog.

I'm aware that Tyler and Corrine have emerged from the bedrooms. They don't speak; they just stare in disbelief as I carefully slip the blade inside RJ's collar and cut it loose.

Corrine speaks. "Oh my GOD."

I drop my body over RJ's, placing my mouth over his. I exhale and watch as his chest begins to rise. His lips are so cold.

"Patrick," Corrine says. "What do you want me to do?"

"Fucking call 911," I say firmly between breaths. I hear myself, but my voice sounds far away. I have no idea what I'm doing.

Tyler is already moving around the apartment hiding paraphernalia. No one is thinking straight. This is all wrong. I hear Corrine speaking with the operator, but she's weeping, and her voice sounds like it's underwater. I'm trying to get RJ's heart beating again, but I've never actually done CPR before except for the classes at the YMCA. I don't know how long I do this, but the siren of the ambulance seems to come quickly. The paramedics push me off of RJ, place a breather over his face, and begin checking his vitals. They tell us that it's best to wait outside so they can work. Tyler is behind me and pulling me to my feet. I notice Rhiannon standing in the hallway with her hand over her mouth. She's not crying, but her glacier-blue eyes seem vacant, and I can see that she's shaking.

"Come on," Tyler says, guiding me outside.

We move from the apartment onto the front porch. A police car arrives, and the officer steps out and tries to separate us, but we're confused and inadvertently ignore him. The girls are still inside. Another cop comes. He whispers something stupid, like "This outta be a lesson to you kids."

Tyler blows up. "What the fuck did he just say?"

I grab him by the arm. "I think we're in enough trouble, Tyler."

I realize how sickly Tyler looks. His eyes are bloodshot and tired looking, his pupils constricted. One of the officers comes out with the girls. They look just as awful.

"Jesus Christ, we look like the walking dead," I murmur.

Tyler's nodding his head. "I don't feel right, man. Do you remember throwing up together last night?"

My mind scrambles to recall. "Yeah. Yeah, I do now. What the fuck did we take?"

"I don't really remember," Tyler answers. "Probably the usual, Xanax...I think I saw some Demerol in there."

"There was Valium on the rug," I tell him.

"That's great," he says with a sigh. "I didn't pick those up, did you?"

"That was the last thing on my mind. Do you think he's gonna be OK?"

Tyler's blue eyes are thick with tears. He hesitates, but before he has a chance to say anything, a cop walks over to us. He asks us our names and what we were up to last night. We tell him that the last thing we remember was being at a keg party at a friend's house.

"Is he gonna be all right?" I ask him.

The cop eyes me hard for a moment. "That young man is dead."

A thick knot is quickly forming in my stomach, and my jaw drops. I'm waiting for the punch line of this sick-ass cop's bad joke, but before he speaks again, the paramedics are wheeling a covered stretcher out of our apartment.

"What happened to your thumb?" the cop asks me.

I glance down at my hands to see what the hell he's talking about, and my thumb is stained red.

"It's RJ's blood. I got his blood on me."

I'm losing it. The world is spinning, and Tyler moves beside me to keep me from collapsing.

The cop continues to question us as the paramedics load RJ into the ambulance. I'm not really paying any attention to the cop; instead, I'm watching the paramedics as they lift the stretcher that carries RJ's lifeless body into the ambulance and close the doors. This is all so surreal. My mind is reeling.

How could I let this happen? First my dad dies and now RJ. What am I gonna tell his parents? His brother? I was supposed to look out for him. I should have done something— known better—Goddammit, Patrick!

A cop dressed in civilian clothes exits our apartment. He hands us his card and says something, but I'm fixated on the ambulance as it drives away. Its lights are flashing, but the siren doesn't come on.

"I'll be in touch," the cop says. "Don't plan on going anywhere before I contact you."

The girls slowly approach us as the cops get into their cars and drive away.

"Oh my God," Corrine says. "He's dead! He's really dead!"

I look to Rhiannon, and she looks completely incoherent.

"What did we take last night?" Tyler asks her.

Rhiannon is dazed; speechless.

Corrine speaks for her. "Morphine."

"Huh?" I manage.

"Pills. You guys were taking all kinds of pills that Rhiannon got from work. You guys took some time-released morphine. I was worried because you guys were acting so funny, but then you threw up, and I figured you were OK."

"Wait," Tyler says. "Did RJ throw up or just us?"

Corrine hesitates before answering. "Um...just you guys that I know of."

Tyler spins away, turning his back to us, and raising his hands to the back of his head.

"I seriously think we're fucking overdosing right now," I say.

"Yeah!" Tyler screams. "And those pigs just fucking *left* us here to *die*! What the *fuck*?"

Rhiannon is trembling so badly that I'm growing more concerned. I'm wondering if she's having a panic attack. She turns and walks back to the front porch and sits, bringing her knees to her chest and burying her head in her arms. Her blonde hair has fallen over her arms, and she finally appears to be crying.

"What the fuck!" I yell. "What are we gonna do? What am I gonna tell his parents?"

"Shame on us!" Tyler screams.

People who live in the apartments near ours are coming outside to see what has happened.

"Hey!" Tyler screams, "why don't you mind your own business? He's fucking dead, OK?"

RJ *is* dead. And while we don't yet realize it, a part of all of us has died with him. We will never be the same. We will never be whole again, and we will never recover from this tragedy.

I will never forgive myself for letting my best friend die. I should have prevented this accident from happening. I should have said that we'd had enough, but I didn't, and now RJ is gone. He's gone forever. He'll never graduate from college or fall in love. He'll never see his little sister again. He'll never have a son of his own or change his diaper or watch him take his first step. He'll never hear his son say, "Da-da," and he'll never have to tell him to be careful and to stay away from drugs because that future's irrelevant now.

RJ's journey has been cut short because we were careless. We had gradually partied more and more, thinking less and less about the risks that we were taking. A life has ended, along with any life that RJ's might eventually have created.

We stumble back inside the apartment and stare at the empty couch. Something catches my eye; RJ's maroon 1969 ball cap is under the couch. I bend down and take it in my hand, and when I stand again, the others see it and begin to cry. This hat is all that's left of RJ now.

I feel an emptiness overcoming me. It's a dark sort of hopelessness—a pain—that reminds me of when my father died in the plane crash a few years ago. I hate this feeling, but I am slowly realizing that I allowed this darkness into my life, and it will never go away.

"Where's the phone?" I whisper numbly. "I need to call his dad."

Epilogue

Two more defendants pleaded guilty Monday to drug charges stemming from the death of their friend last year. A third defendant had already pleaded guilty, while a deal for the fourth defendant was still pending.

The four defendants—Patrick Mitchell, Tyler Hammond, Corrine Brunsfield, and Rhiannon Bell—were facing charges of drug possession and other related misdemeanors after they had reported that they found their friend, RJ Scott, had died after a long night of partying that involved binge-drinking and the abuse of prescription drugs.

Ms. Bell, a nursing student, has admitted to law enforcement that she stole 100-milligram, time-release morphine tablets from the pharmacy where she worked, and passed them out to the group on May 15, 2001.

Everyone who had taken one of the pills became ill and vomited the heavy dosage of medication, with the exception of RJ Scott, 21, who passed out and died.

No one had been charged with the death of the victim, a decision that had upset his family. According to Assistant District Attorney Samantha Winthrop, there was still a possibility that Ms. Bell would face more severe charges.

Ms. Brunsfield pleaded guilty last month to several drug charges. She will be required to serve two years of probation, substance abuse treatment, and 100 hours of community service.

Mr. Hammond and Mr. Mitchell pleaded guilty to drug charges on

Monday. Both of the young men received 90-day prison sentences that were suspended pending two years of supervised probation. Additionally, the young men will undergo substance abuse evaluations and treatment, pay $400 each in restitution in fines, and perform 32 hours of community service.

The defense attorney who represents the four defendants said that they "are so sorry about the death of their friend. They made no excuses for their conduct."

About the Author

Aaron Powell served as a marine during Operation Iraqi Freedom and Operation Enduring Freedom. He graduated from the University of North Carolina at Wilmington in 2003 with a BA in criminal justice and a psychology minor. He also completed a second BA in business administration at Ashford University, where he graduated with distinction in 2011. Aaron Powell is a prolific writer, an avid reader, and is an active marksman. Aaron and his wife and sons live near Austin, Texas.